YOUR DREAMS AND YOU
JOURNAL & PLANNER

52-Week Undated Agenda
and Dream Journal

Also by Ivania Alvarado:

*Your Dreams and You
(English and Spanish Editions)
IvaniaAlvarado.com
sfsre.net*

Your Dreams and You Journal & Planner
First English Edition
ISBN: 978-1-737560203

© 2021 by Ivania Alvarado
All rights reserved. No part of this book may be used or reproduced by any means, graphic, electronic, or mechanical, stored in a database including photocopying, recording, taping or by any information storage retrieval system without the written permission of the publisher except in the case of brief quotations embodied in critical articles and reviews.

This Journal & Planner Belongs to:

Name: _____

Address: _____

City/State & Zip: _____

Phone: _____

Email: _____

Website: _____

Social Media:

Facebook: _____

Instagram: _____

Twitter: _____

YouTube: _____

Pinterest: _____

Contacts

Dream Catcher History & Legend

Dream catchers are one of the most fascinating traditions of Native Americans. The traditional dream catcher was intended to protect the sleeping individual from negative dreams, while letting positive dreams through. The positive dreams would slip through the hole in the center of the dream catcher, and glide down the feathers to the sleeping person below. The negative dreams would get caught up in the web, and expire when the first rays of the sun struck them.

The dream catcher has been a part of Native American culture for generations. One element of Native American dream catcher relates to the tradition of the hoop. Some Native Americans of North America held the hoop in the highest esteem, because it symbolized strength and unity. Many symbols started around the hoop, and one of these symbols is the dream catcher.

Dream Catcher Lore:

Native Americans believe that the night air is filled with dreams both good and bad. The dream catcher when hung over or near your bed swinging freely in the air, catches the dreams as they flow by. The good dreams know how to pass through the dream catcher, slipping through the outer holes and slide down the soft feathers so gently that many times the sleeper does not know that he/she is dreaming. The bad dreams not knowing the way get tangled in the dream catcher and perish with the first light of the new day.

How the Dream Catcher is made:

Using a hoop of willow, and decorating it with findings, bits and pieces of everyday life, (feathers, arrow heads, beads, etc) the dream catcher is believed to have the power to catch all of a person's dreams, trapping the bad ones, and letting only the good dreams pass through the dream catcher.

Dreams diary and its use

Dear Dreamers,

I would like this diary to be useful so you can learn and practice for yourself the interpretation of your dreams.

It's a day diary so you can start your own interpretations, and create a positive habit.

If for any reason you don't remember your dream, you can start by writing how you feel when you wake up, that is the first step to remember, it's an exercise that with time you'll learn.

Remember there are many reasons as to why keeping a diary of your dreams is important:

- You can have a millionaire idea.
- You'll have a better connection with yourself.
- You'll know yourself better.
- Your conscience and subconscious will be aligned more easily when they face each other.
- You'll be able to heal past wounds.
- Decipher messages.
- Your dreams always work in your favor, make them work for you.
- Improves memory.
- Most will be fun to relive.
- It'll be something else to share with your friends and family.
- For some it works like therapy.
- Warnings of any adversity.
- Improves creativity.
- You can evaluate your feelings.
- It's an exercise for your mind.

And much more...

Secrets for your dreams diary to be successful

Title your dream, try to make it coincide and describe in a few words what you've dreamed, example: "Dream was about yellow shoes."

Place the exact date of the dream, as well as the hour.

Write how you feel when you wake up.

Include pictures or drawings if you have them. For example, if you have dreamed of a deceased family member, it's great if you can include a picture of that person.

Describe your feelings and sensations and ambience during the dream, use very descriptive words, include details, did it rain, was it cold, was it a sunny day, etc.

Describe if the dream refers to past situations or future.

Try to remember the dialogues or if you heard or think you heard voices with messages that communicated something special.

Describe the people in the dream, if they were family members, friends or if they were strangers.

Control your mind before going to sleep, perform small rituals that allow you to achieve a deep, healing and enjoyable sleep.

And remember, by interpreting your dreams with the tools and strategies I've given you, you can make dreams come true.

2022

January
S	M	T	W	T	F	S
30	31					1
2	3	4	5	6	7	8
9	10	11	12	13	14	15
16	17	18	19	20	21	22
23	24	25	26	27	28	29

February
S	M	T	W	T	F	S
		1	2	3	4	5
6	7	8	9	10	11	12
13	14	15	16	17	18	19
20	21	22	23	24	25	26
27	28					

March
S	M	T	W	T	F	S
		1	2	3	4	5
6	7	8	9	10	11	12
13	14	15	16	17	18	19
20	21	22	23	24	25	26
27	28	29	30	31		

April
S	M	T	W	T	F	S
					1	2
3	4	5	6	7	8	9
10	11	12	13	14	15	16
17	18	19	20	21	22	23
24	25	26	27	28	29	30

May
S	M	T	W	T	F	S
1	2	3	4	5	6	7
8	9	10	11	12	13	14
15	16	17	18	19	20	21
22	23	24	25	26	27	28
29	30	31				

June
S	M	T	W	T	F	S
			1	2	3	4
5	6	7	8	9	10	11
12	13	14	15	16	17	18
19	20	21	22	23	24	25
26	27	28	29	30		

July
S	M	T	W	T	F	S
31					1	2
3	4	5	6	7	8	9
10	11	12	13	14	15	16
17	18	19	20	21	22	23
24	25	26	27	28	29	30

August
S	M	T	W	T	F	S
	1	2	3	4	5	6
7	8	9	10	11	12	13
14	15	16	17	18	19	20
21	22	23	24	25	26	27
28	29	30	31			

September
S	M	T	W	T	F	S
				1	2	3
4	5	6	7	8	9	10
11	12	13	14	15	16	17
18	19	20	21	22	23	24
25	26	27	28	29	30	

October
S	M	T	W	T	F	S
30	31					1
2	3	4	5	6	7	8
9	10	11	12	13	14	15
16	17	18	19	20	21	22
23	24	25	26	27	28	29

November
S	M	T	W	T	F	S
		1	2	3	4	5
6	7	8	9	10	11	12
13	14	15	16	17	18	19
20	21	22	23	24	25	26
27	28	29	30			

December
S	M	T	W	T	F	S
				1	2	3
4	5	6	7	8	9	10
11	12	13	14	15	16	17
18	19	20	21	22	23	24
25	26	27	28	29	30	31

2023

January
S	M	T	W	T	F	S
1	2	3	4	5	6	7
8	9	10	11	12	13	14
15	16	17	18	19	20	21
22	23	24	25	26	27	28
29	30	31				

February
S	M	T	W	T	F	S
			1	2	3	4
5	6	7	8	9	10	11
12	13	14	15	16	17	18
19	20	21	22	23	24	25
26	27	28				

March
S	M	T	W	T	F	S
			1	2	3	4
5	6	7	8	9	10	11
12	13	14	15	16	17	18
19	20	21	22	23	24	25
26	27	28	29	30	31	

April
S	M	T	W	T	F	S
30						1
2	3	4	5	6	7	8
9	10	11	12	13	14	15
16	17	18	19	20	21	22
23	24	25	26	27	28	29

May
S	M	T	W	T	F	S
	1	2	3	4	5	6
7	8	9	10	11	12	13
14	15	16	17	18	19	20
21	22	23	24	25	26	27
28	29	30	31			

June
S	M	T	W	T	F	S
				1	2	3
4	5	6	7	8	9	10
11	12	13	14	15	16	17
18	19	20	21	22	23	24
25	26	27	28	29	30	

July
S	M	T	W	T	F	S
30	31					1
2	3	4	5	6	7	8
9	10	11	12	13	14	15
16	17	18	19	20	21	22
23	24	25	26	27	28	29

August
S	M	T	W	T	F	S
		1	2	3	4	5
6	7	8	9	10	11	12
13	14	15	16	17	18	19
20	21	22	23	24	25	26
27	28	29	30	31		

September
S	M	T	W	T	F	S
					1	2
3	4	5	6	7	8	9
10	11	12	13	14	15	16
17	18	19	20	21	22	23
24	25	26	27	28	29	30

October
S	M	T	W	T	F	S
1	2	3	4	5	6	7
8	9	10	11	12	13	14
15	16	17	18	19	20	21
22	23	24	25	26	27	28
29	30	31				

November
S	M	T	W	T	F	S
			1	2	3	4
5	6	7	8	9	10	11
12	13	14	15	16	17	18
19	20	21	22	23	24	25
26	27	28	29	30		

December
S	M	T	W	T	F	S
31					1	2
3	4	5	6	7	8	9
10	11	12	13	14	15	16
17	18	19	20	21	22	23
24	25	26	27	28	29	30

2024

January
S	M	T	W	T	F	S
	1	2	3	4	5	6
7	8	9	10	11	12	13
14	15	16	17	18	19	20
21	22	23	24	25	26	27
28	29	30	31			

February
S	M	T	W	T	F	S
				1	2	3
4	5	6	7	8	9	10
11	12	13	14	15	16	17
18	19	20	21	22	23	24
25	26	27	28	29		

March
S	M	T	W	T	F	S
31					1	2
3	4	5	6	7	8	9
10	11	12	13	14	15	16
17	18	19	20	21	22	23
24	25	26	27	28	29	30

April
S	M	T	W	T	F	S
	1	2	3	4	5	6
7	8	9	10	11	12	13
14	15	16	17	18	19	20
21	22	23	24	25	26	27
28	29	30				

May
S	M	T	W	T	F	S
			1	2	3	4
5	6	7	8	9	10	11
12	13	14	15	16	17	18
19	20	21	22	23	24	25
26	27	28	29	30	31	

June
S	M	T	W	T	F	S
30						1
2	3	4	5	6	7	8
9	10	11	12	13	14	15
16	17	18	19	20	21	22
23	24	25	26	27	28	29

July
S	M	T	W	T	F	S
	1	2	3	4	5	6
7	8	9	10	11	12	13
14	15	16	17	18	19	20
21	22	23	24	25	26	27
28	29	30	31			

August
S	M	T	W	T	F	S
				1	2	3
4	5	6	7	8	9	10
11	12	13	14	15	16	17
18	19	20	21	22	23	24
25	26	27	28	29	30	31

September
S	M	T	W	T	F	S
1	2	3	4	5	6	7
8	9	10	11	12	13	14
15	16	17	18	19	20	21
22	23	24	25	26	27	28
29	30					

October
S	M	T	W	T	F	S
		1	2	3	4	5
6	7	8	9	10	11	12
13	14	15	16	17	18	19
20	21	22	23	24	25	26
27	28	29	30	31		

November
S	M	T	W	T	F	S
					1	2
3	4	5	6	7	8	9
10	11	12	13	14	15	16
17	18	19	20	21	22	23
24	25	26	27	28	29	30

December
S	M	T	W	T	F	S
1	2	3	4	5	6	7
8	9	10	11	12	13	14
15	16	17	18	19	20	21
22	23	24	25	26	27	28
29	30	31				

2025

January
S	M	T	W	T	F	S
			1	2	3	4
5	6	7	8	9	10	11
12	13	14	15	16	17	18
19	20	21	22	23	24	25
26	27	28	29	30	31	

February
S	M	T	W	T	F	S
						1
2	3	4	5	6	7	8
9	10	11	12	13	14	15
16	17	18	19	20	21	22
23	24	25	26	27	28	

March
S	M	T	W	T	F	S
30	31					1
2	3	4	5	6	7	8
9	10	11	12	13	14	15
16	17	18	19	20	21	22
23	24	25	26	27	28	29

April
S	M	T	W	T	F	S
		1	2	3	4	5
6	7	8	9	10	11	12
13	14	15	16	17	18	19
20	21	22	23	24	25	26
27	28	29	30			

May
S	M	T	W	T	F	S
				1	2	3
4	5	6	7	8	9	10
11	12	13	14	15	16	17
18	19	20	21	22	23	24
25	26	27	28	29	30	31

June
S	M	T	W	T	F	S
1	2	3	4	5	6	7
8	9	10	11	12	13	14
15	16	17	18	19	20	21
22	23	24	25	26	27	28
29	30					

July
S	M	T	W	T	F	S
		1	2	3	4	5
6	7	8	9	10	11	12
13	14	15	16	17	18	19
20	21	22	23	24	25	26
27	28	29	30	31		

August
S	M	T	W	T	F	S
31					1	2
3	4	5	6	7	8	9
10	11	12	13	14	15	16
17	18	19	20	21	22	23
24	25	26	27	28	29	30

September
S	M	T	W	T	F	S
	1	2	3	4	5	6
7	8	9	10	11	12	13
14	15	16	17	18	19	20
21	22	23	24	25	26	27
28	29	30				

October
S	M	T	W	T	F	S
			1	2	3	4
5	6	7	8	9	10	11
12	13	14	15	16	17	18
19	20	21	22	23	24	25
26	27	28	29	30	31	

November
S	M	T	W	T	F	S
30						1
2	3	4	5	6	7	8
9	10	11	12	13	14	15
16	17	18	19	20	21	22
23	24	25	26	27	28	29

December
S	M	T	W	T	F	S
	1	2	3	4	5	6
7	8	9	10	11	12	13
14	15	16	17	18	19	20
21	22	23	24	25	26	27
28	29	30	31			

Month: _____

Monthly Calendar

TO-DO LIST:

NOTES:

This Month's Focus:

Your Dreams and You Journal & Planner

MONDAY

TUESDAY

WEDNESDAY

☐ Things to Do:

☐ Things to Do:

☐ Things to Do:

FEELING UPON AWAKENING:
Happy ☐
Sad ☐
Angry ☐
Other: _____

SKETCH YOUR DREAM

Weekly Planner

THURSDAY

FRIDAY

SATURDAY

☐ Things to Do:
☐
☐
☐

SUNDAY

☐ Things to Do:
☐
☐
☐
☐
☐
☐

☐ Things to Do:
☐
☐
☐
☐
☐
☐

☐ Things to Do:
☐
☐
☐

*ABUNDANCE: Seeing yourself in abundance is good if you wake up happy. It means you'll have more. If you wake up sad, you are afraid of losing your wealth. You will have difficulties with your finances. If you are not wealthy, it is a fortunate message for your finances. LN*12359, (2)*

NOTES

Your Dreams and You Journal & Planner

MONDAY

TUESDAY

WEDNESDAY

☐ Things to Do:
☐
☐
☐
☐
☐
☐

☐ Things to Do:
☐
☐
☐
☐
☐
☐

☐ Things to Do:
☐
☐
☐
☐
☐
☐

FEELING UPON AWAKENING:
Happy ☐
Sad ☐
Angry ☐
Other: _____
_____

SKETCH YOUR DREAM

Weekly Planner

THURSDAY
☐

FRIDAY
☐

SATURDAY
☐

☐ Things to Do:
☐
☐
☐

SUNDAY
☐

☐ Things to Do:
☐
☐
☐
☐
☐

☐ Things to Do:
☐
☐
☐
☐
☐
☐

*ANCESTORS: Since they are no longer with you, generally they reappear to reveal enigmas or solutions. If you are not behaving well, they will reappear so you can explain your behavior. If you don't change, they will come back. LN*15351, (6)*

☐ Things to Do:
☐
☐
☐

NOTES

| 15

Your Dreams and You Journal & Planner

MONDAY

TUESDAY

WEDNESDAY

☐ Things to Do:

☐ Things to Do:

☐ Things to Do:

FEELING UPON AWAKENING:
Happy ☐
Sad ☐
Angry ☐
Other: _____

SKETCH YOUR DREAM

16

Weekly Planner

THURSDAY
☐

FRIDAY
☐

SATURDAY
☐

☐ Things to Do:
☐
☐
☐

SUNDAY
☐

☐ Things to Do:
☐
☐
☐
☐
☐
☐

☐ Things to Do:
☐
☐
☐
☐
☐
☐

*ANGEL: It is always good to dream about angels, whether you're dreaming about one angel or many. Having good relationships with them is better. Good times are coming. LN*15753, (21)*

☐ Things to Do:
☐
☐
☐

NOTES

Your Dreams and You Journal & Planner

MONDAY	TUESDAY	WEDNESDAY

☐ Things to Do:	☐ Things to Do:	☐ Things to Do:

FEELING UPON AWAKENING:
Happy ☐
Sad ☐
Angry ☐
Other: _____

SKETCH YOUR DREAM

Weekly Planner

THURSDAY

FRIDAY

SATURDAY

☐ Things to Do:
☐
☐
☐

SUNDAY

☐ Things to Do:
☐
☐
☐
☐
☐
☐

☐ Things to Do:
☐
☐
☐
☐
☐
☐

*ARTIST: You admire or wish to be anything like the artist in a professional aspect. You will be on a stage, in an artistic way, a new life path, or changes in your work. It also means flattery. LN*19293, (6)*

☐ Things to Do:
☐
☐
☐

NOTES

Your Dreams and You Journal & Planner

MONDAY

TUESDAY

WEDNESDAY

☐ Things to Do:

☐ Things to Do:

☐ Things to Do:

FEELING UPON AWAKENING:
Happy ☐
Sad ☐
Angry ☐
Other: _____

SKETCH YOUR DREAM

Weekly Planner

THURSDAY

☐

FRIDAY

☐

SATURDAY

☐

☐ Things to Do:
☐
☐
☐

SUNDAY

☐

☐ Things to Do:
☐
☐
☐
☐
☐
☐

☐ Things to Do:
☐
☐
☐
☐
☐

BABY: It's bad luck to see a defenseless baby who can't fend for itself; you will have some complications but they will be resolved. If the baby is sick there might be someone in serious condition in your family. If the child is a little bit older and robust, this is good luck. LN*2127, (3)

☐ Things to Do:
☐
☐
☐

NOTES

Your Dreams and You Journal & Planner

Month: _____

Monthly Calendar

TO-DO LIST:

NOTES:

This Month's Focus:

Your Dreams and You Journal & Planner

MONDAY ☐	TUESDAY ☐	WEDNESDAY ☐

☐ Things to Do: ☐ Things to Do: ☐ Things to Do:

FEELING UPON AWAKENING:
Happy ☐
Sad ☐
Angry ☐
Other: _____

SKETCH YOUR DREAM

Weekly Planner

THURSDAY

FRIDAY

SATURDAY

☐ Things to Do:
☐
☐
☐

SUNDAY

☐ Things to Do:
☐
☐
☐
☐
☐
☐

☐ Things to Do:
☐
☐
☐
☐
☐
☐

☐ Things to Do:
☐
☐
☐

*BAREFOOT: Related to hard work and difficulties that you will only resolve with perseverance. If you see yourself walking barefoot on a rocky path, you have a long way to go before getting to where you want. Have patience and don't give up. LN*21952, (1)*

NOTES

Your Dreams and You Journal & Planner

MONDAY

TUESDAY

WEDNESDAY

☐ Things to Do:

☐ Things to Do:

☐ Things to Do:

FEELING UPON AWAKENING:
Happy ☐
Sad ☐
Angry ☐
Other: _____

SKETCH YOUR DREAM

Weekly Planner

THURSDAY

FRIDAY

SATURDAY

☐ Things to Do:
☐
☐
☐

SUNDAY

☐ Things to Do:
☐ Things to Do:

*BEES: This is a good sign in any matter, and more so in matters of money, property, and improvement for those who have it. If they sting you, you will have some difficulties. If you kill them you will have improvement. LN*2551, (4)*

NOTES

☐ Things to Do:
☐
☐
☐

Your Dreams and You Journal & Planner

MONDAY

TUESDAY

WEDNESDAY

☐ Things to Do:
☐
☐
☐
☐
☐
☐

☐ Things to Do:
☐
☐
☐
☐
☐
☐

☐ Things to Do:
☐
☐
☐
☐
☐
☐

FEELING UPON AWAKENING:
Happy ☐
Sad ☐
Angry ☐
Other: _____
_____

SKETCH YOUR DREAM

Weekly Planner

THURSDAY
☐

FRIDAY
☐

SATURDAY
☐

☐ Things to Do:
☐
☐
☐

SUNDAY
☐

☐ Things to Do:
☐
☐
☐
☐
☐
☐

☐ Things to Do:
☐
☐
☐
☐
☐
☐

*BIRTH: The start of everything in life. You're in a new project. Abundance if you're married. If you see yourself as a single mom, you'll go through problems. If you're happy being a single mom, you'll do well. LN*29928, (3)*

☐ Things to Do:
☐
☐
☐

NOTES

Your Dreams and You Journal & Planner

MONDAY

TUESDAY

WEDNESDAY

☐ Things to Do:
☐
☐
☐
☐
☐
☐

☐ Things to Do:
☐
☐
☐
☐
☐
☐

☐ Things to Do:
☐
☐
☐
☐
☐
☐

FEELING UPON AWAKENING:
Happy ☐
Sad ☐
Angry ☐
Other: _____
_____

SKETCH YOUR DREAM

Weekly Planner

THURSDAY

FRIDAY

SATURDAY

☐ Things to Do:

SUNDAY

☐ Things to Do:

☐ Things to Do:

☐ Things to Do:

*BLOOD: The interpretation depends on how the dream goes on. What does blood represent for you? If you're scared, it's a negative result in your health or mood. If your reaction is positive, it's good in various areas including love. LN*23664, (3)*

NOTES

Your Dreams and You Journal & Planner

MONDAY

TUESDAY

WEDNESDAY

☐ Things to Do:
☐
☐
☐
☐
☐
☐

☐ Things to Do:
☐
☐
☐
☐
☐
☐

☐ Things to Do:
☐
☐
☐
☐
☐
☐

FEELING UPON AWAKENING:
Happy ☐
Sad ☐
Angry ☐
Other: _____
_____

SKETCH YOUR DREAM

Weekly Planner

THURSDAY
☐

FRIDAY
☐

SATURDAY
☐

☐ Things to Do:
☐
☐
☐

SUNDAY
☐

☐ Things to Do:
☐
☐
☐
☐
☐
☐

☐ Things to Do:
☐
☐
☐
☐
☐
☐

*BOSS: It depends on the relationship you have currently with your boss. Usually the dream reveals delicate situations with your job that have nothing to do with love. LN*2611, (1)*

NOTES

☐ Things to Do:
☐
☐
☐

Your Dreams and You Journal & Planner

Month: _____

Monthly Calendar

TO-DO LIST:

NOTES:

This Month's Focus:

Your Dreams and You Journal & Planner

MONDAY   TUESDAY   WEDNESDAY

☐ Things to Do: ☐ Things to Do: ☐ Things to Do:

FEELING UPON AWAKENING:
Happy ☐
Sad ☐
Angry ☐
Other: _____
_____

SKETCH YOUR DREAM

Weekly Planner

THURSDAY

FRIDAY

SATURDAY

☐ Things to Do:
☐
☐
☐

SUNDAY

☐ Things to Do:
☐
☐
☐
☐
☐
☐

☐ Things to Do:
☐
☐
☐
☐
☐
☐

*BUTTERFLY: Good news. It means metamorphosis, whether it's you or someone else, depending on the dream. If you see butterflies in the daytime, it's a good sign, especially if they are colorful and bright. LN*23223, (9)*

NOTES

☐ Things to Do:
☐
☐
☐

Your Dreams and You Journal & Planner

MONDAY

TUESDAY

WEDNESDAY

☐ Things to Do:

☐ Things to Do:

☐ Things to Do:

FEELING UPON AWAKENING:
Happy ☐
Sad ☐
Angry ☐
Other: _____

SKETCH YOUR DREAM

Weekly Planner

THURSDAY

FRIDAY

SATURDAY

☐ Things to Do:
☐
☐
☐

SUNDAY

☐ Things to Do:
☐ Things to Do:

*CAT: It's femininity, intuition, and magic. Also, depending on the color of the cat, it can alter the meaning of the dream. LN*312, (6)*

☐ Things to Do:
☐
☐
☐

NOTES

Your Dreams and You Journal & Planner

MONDAY

TUESDAY

WEDNESDAY

☐ Things to Do:

☐ Things to Do:

☐ Things to Do:

FEELING UPON AWAKENING:
Happy ☐
Sad ☐
Angry ☐
Other: _____

SKETCH YOUR DREAM

Weekly Planner

THURSDAY

FRIDAY

SATURDAY

☐ Things to Do:

SUNDAY

☐ Things to Do:

☐ Things to Do:

*CHILDREN: When you dream about your son it refers to your daughter, and vice versa. If you dream about your adult kids as babies, you want to make up for lost time. If you don't have a good relationship, it's time to see what you've failed in and repair it. LN*38935, (1)*

NOTES

☐ Things to Do:

Your Dreams and You Journal & Planner

MONDAY

TUESDAY

WEDNESDAY

☐ Things to Do:
- ☐
- ☐
- ☐
- ☐
- ☐
- ☐

☐ Things to Do:
- ☐
- ☐
- ☐
- ☐
- ☐
- ☐

☐ Things to Do:
- ☐
- ☐
- ☐
- ☐
- ☐
- ☐

FEELING UPON AWAKENING:
Happy ☐
Sad ☐
Angry ☐
Other: _____

SKETCH YOUR DREAM

Weekly Planner

THURSDAY
☐

FRIDAY
☐

SATURDAY
☐

☐ Things to Do:
☐
☐
☐

SUNDAY
☐

☐ Things to Do:
☐
☐
☐
☐
☐
☐

☐ Things to Do:
☐
☐
☐
☐
☐

*CHRISTMAS: Happiness and union in the family. If there are many lights on the Christmas tree, it means growth and improvement. LN*38999, (11)*

☐ Things to Do:
☐
☐
☐

NOTES

Your Dreams and You Journal & Planner

MONDAY

TUESDAY

WEDNESDAY

☐ Things to Do:
☐
☐
☐
☐
☐
☐

☐ Things to Do:
☐
☐
☐
☐
☐
☐

☐ Things to Do:
☐
☐
☐
☐
☐
☐

FEELING UPON AWAKENING:
Happy ☐
Sad ☐
Angry ☐
Other: _____

SKETCH YOUR DREAM

Weekly Planner

THURSDAY

FRIDAY

SATURDAY

☐ Things to Do:

SUNDAY

☐ Things to Do:

☐ Things to Do:

*CLOUDS: Internal peace, it reflects a dreamer who dreams when awake. It's a projection towards your future, the way you will reach your objective, even if sometimes you must come down to Earth. LN*33635, (2)*

☐ Things to Do:

NOTES

Month: _____

Monthly Calendar

TO-DO LIST:

NOTES:

This Month's Focus:

Your Dreams and You Journal & Planner

MONDAY   TUESDAY   WEDNESDAY

☐ Things to Do: ☐ Things to Do: ☐ Things to Do:

FEELING UPON AWAKENING:
Happy ☐
Sad ☐
Angry ☐
Other: _____

SKETCH YOUR DREAM

Weekly Planner

THURSDAY

FRIDAY

SATURDAY

☐ Things to Do:
☐
☐
☐

SUNDAY

☐ Things to Do:
☐
☐
☐
☐
☐
☐

☐ Things to Do:
☐
☐
☐
☐
☐
☐

☐ Things to Do:
☐
☐
☐

*COFFEE: Seeing yourself grinding the coffee means strength of character. Coffee beans mean fortune and intellect. If the coffee spills, it means setbacks. LN*36661, (4)*

NOTES

Your Dreams and You Journal & Planner

MONDAY

TUESDAY

WEDNESDAY

☐ Things to Do:

☐ Things to Do:

☐ Things to Do:

FEELING UPON AWAKENING:
Happy ☐
Sad ☐
Angry ☐
Other: _____

SKETCH YOUR DREAM

Weekly Planner

THURSDAY

FRIDAY

SATURDAY

☐ Things to Do:
☐
☐
☐

SUNDAY

☐ Things to Do:
☐
☐
☐
☐
☐
☐

☐ Things to Do:
☐
☐
☐
☐
☐
☐

*CRYING: If you're crying because of mishaps, there will be drastic changes in your life and you'll have big complications. If it's not because of mishaps, it means the contrary. LN*39793, (4)*

☐ Things to Do:
☐
☐
☐

NOTES

Your Dreams and You Journal & Planner

MONDAY

TUESDAY

WEDNESDAY

☐ Things to Do:
☐
☐
☐
☐
☐
☐

☐ Things to Do:
☐
☐
☐
☐
☐
☐

☐ Things to Do:
☐
☐
☐
☐
☐
☐

FEELING UPON AWAKENING:
Happy ☐
Sad ☐
Angry ☐
Other: _____
_____

SKETCH YOUR DREAM

52

Weekly Planner

THURSDAY
☐

FRIDAY
☐

SATURDAY
☐

☐ Things to Do:
☐
☐
☐

SUNDAY
☐

☐ Things to Do:
☐
☐
☐
☐
☐
☐

☐ Things to Do:
☐
☐
☐
☐
☐

*DANCING: It's fortunate to see yourself dancing in your own house. If it's a costume dance, beware of lies and stop being so fake. Dancing with a woman means fear of the opposite sex. Dancing between men is fear of falling in love with another man. LN*41533, (7)*

NOTES

Your Dreams and You Journal & Planner

MONDAY ## TUESDAY ## WEDNESDAY

☐ Things to Do:
- ☐
- ☐
- ☐
- ☐
- ☐
- ☐

☐ Things to Do:
- ☐
- ☐
- ☐
- ☐
- ☐
- ☐

☐ Things to Do:
- ☐
- ☐
- ☐
- ☐
- ☐
- ☐

<u>FEELING UPON AWAKENING</u>:
Happy ☐
Sad ☐
Angry ☐
Other: _____
_____

SKETCH YOUR DREAM

Weekly Planner

THURSDAY

FRIDAY

SATURDAY

☐ Things to Do:

SUNDAY

☐ Things to Do:

☐ Things to Do:

*DRAGON: Happiness and fortune. If the dragon tries to attack you with fire, it means disappointment in love. LN*49172, (5)*

☐ Things to Do:

NOTES

Your Dreams and You Journal & Planner

MONDAY

TUESDAY

WEDNESDAY

☐ Things to Do:
☐
☐
☐
☐
☐
☐

☐ Things to Do:
☐
☐
☐
☐
☐
☐

☐ Things to Do:
☐
☐
☐
☐
☐
☐

FEELING UPON AWAKENING:
Happy ☐
Sad ☐
Angry ☐
Other: _____

SKETCH YOUR DREAM

Weekly Planner

THURSDAY

FRIDAY

SATURDAY

☐ Things to Do:

SUNDAY

☐ Things to Do:

☐ Things to Do:

☐ Things to Do:

DOG: The dog can represent a loved one. It could also mean someone isn't being loyal to you. LN*467, (8)

NOTES

| 57

Month: _____

Monthly Calendar

TO-DO LIST:

NOTES:

This Month's Focus:

Your Dreams and You Journal & Planner

MONDAY TUESDAY WEDNESDAY

☐ Things to Do: ☐ Things to Do: ☐ Things to Do:

FEELING UPON AWAKENING:
Happy ☐
Sad ☐
Angry ☐
Other: _____

SKETCH YOUR DREAM

Weekly Planner

THURSDAY

FRIDAY

SATURDAY

☐ Things to Do:
☐
☐
☐

SUNDAY

☐ Things to Do:
☐ Things to Do:

☐ Things to Do:
☐
☐
☐

ELEPHANT: If you see the elephant healthy and free, it means good fortune, new and important friendships, noble friends, and freedom. If the elephant is encaged, danger. LN*53577, (9)

NOTES

Your Dreams and You Journal & Planner

MONDAY

TUESDAY

WEDNESDAY

☐ Things to Do:

☐ Things to Do:

☐ Things to Do:

FEELING UPON AWAKENING:
Happy ☐
Sad ☐
Angry ☐
Other: _____

SKETCH YOUR DREAM

Weekly Planner

THURSDAY
☐

FRIDAY
☐

SATURDAY
☐

☐ Things to Do:
☐
☐
☐

SUNDAY
☐

☐ Things to Do:
☐
☐
☐
☐
☐
☐

☐ Things to Do:
☐
☐
☐
☐
☐
☐

*FACTORY: Working factory, you will have fortune in your business and financial plans. Abandoned factory, failure. Little activity in the factory, losses. LN*61324, (7)*

☐ Things to Do:
☐
☐
☐

NOTES

Your Dreams and You Journal & Planner

MONDAY

TUESDAY

WEDNESDAY

☐ Things to Do:

☐ Things to Do:

☐ Things to Do:

FEELING UPON AWAKENING:
Happy ☐
Sad ☐
Angry ☐
Other: _____
_____

SKETCH YOUR DREAM

Weekly Planner

THURSDAY

FRIDAY

SATURDAY

☐ Things to Do:

SUNDAY

☐ Things to Do:

☐ Things to Do:

☐ Things to Do:

*FEAR: If you face your fear and find out why you're scared you'll resolve anything you have yet to resolve. It means defeat if you don't face it. If you wake up with the fear, you'll have a problem that's hard to face. LN*6519, (21)*

NOTES

Your Dreams and You Journal & Planner

MONDAY ☐	TUESDAY ☐	WEDNESDAY ☐

☐ Things to Do:
☐
☐
☐
☐
☐
☐

☐ Things to Do:
☐
☐
☐
☐
☐
☐

☐ Things to Do:
☐
☐
☐
☐
☐
☐

FEELING UPON AWAKENING:
Happy ☐
Sad ☐
Angry ☐
Other: _____

SKETCH YOUR DREAM

Weekly Planner

THURSDAY

FRIDAY

SATURDAY

☐ Things to Do:

SUNDAY

☐ Things to Do:

☐ Things to Do:

FLOWERS: Great bliss if you receive them. It's a good sign to see flowers. Red flowers mean you are in love; white flowers mean peace and happiness in the family. LN*63656, (8)

☐ Things to Do:

NOTES

Your Dreams and You Journal & Planner

MONDAY

TUESDAY

WEDNESDAY

☐ Things to Do:
- ☐
- ☐
- ☐
- ☐
- ☐
- ☐

☐ Things to Do:
- ☐
- ☐
- ☐
- ☐
- ☐
- ☐

☐ Things to Do:
- ☐
- ☐
- ☐
- ☐
- ☐
- ☐

FEELING UPON AWAKENING:
Happy ☐
Sad ☐
Angry ☐
Other: _____
_____

SKETCH YOUR DREAM

Weekly Planner

THURSDAY

FRIDAY

SATURDAY

☐ Things to Do:
☐
☐
☐

SUNDAY

☐ Things to Do:
☐
☐
☐
☐
☐

☐ Things to Do:
☐
☐
☐
☐
☐

FOREST: If you're alone in the forest, it's good luck in everything. If someone is with you, it means possible deception. Beautiful big trees mean abundance. If you want to get out of the forest but can't, it means obstacles. LN*66953, (11)

☐ Things to Do:
☐
☐
☐

NOTES

Your Dreams and You Journal & Planner

Month: _____

Monthly Calendar

TO-DO LIST:

NOTES:

This Month's Focus:

Your Dreams and You Journal & Planner

MONDAY	TUESDAY	WEDNESDAY

☐ Things to Do: ☐ Things to Do: ☐ Things to Do:

FEELING UPON AWAKENING:
Happy ☐
Sad ☐
Angry ☐
Other: _____

SKETCH YOUR DREAM

Weekly Planner

THURSDAY
☐

FRIDAY
☐

SATURDAY
☐

☐ Things to Do:
☐
☐
☐

SUNDAY
☐

☐ Things to Do:
☐
☐
☐
☐
☐
☐

☐ Things to Do:
☐
☐
☐
☐
☐
☐

GOLD: Gold is a precious metal that balances your personality. Speaks to your need for power and ambition. If you have something golden on, it means luck in your life. LN*7634, (2)

☐ Things to Do:
☐
☐
☐

NOTES

Your Dreams and You Journal & Planner

MONDAY

TUESDAY

WEDNESDAY

_____ | _____ | _____

☐ Things to Do:
☐ _____
☐ _____
☐ _____
☐ _____
☐ _____
☐ _____

☐ Things to Do:
☐ _____
☐ _____
☐ _____
☐ _____
☐ _____
☐ _____

☐ Things to Do:
☐ _____
☐ _____
☐ _____
☐ _____
☐ _____
☐ _____

<u>FEELING UPON AWAKENING</u>:
Happy ☐
Sad ☐
Angry ☐
Other: _____
_____

SKETCH YOUR DREAM

Weekly Planner

THURSDAY
☐

FRIDAY
☐

SATURDAY
☐

☐ Things to Do:
☐
☐
☐

SUNDAY
☐

☐ Things to Do:
☐
☐
☐
☐
☐
☐

☐ Things to Do:
☐
☐
☐
☐
☐

*GRAPES: A signal of prosperity and wealth. White grapes are a good sign, especially for sick people. Black grapes mean destabilization and the wrong use of money. LN*79176, (3)*

☐ Things to Do:
☐
☐
☐

NOTES

Your Dreams and You Journal & Planner

MONDAY

TUESDAY

WEDNESDAY

☐ Things to Do:

☐ Things to Do:

☐ Things to Do:

FEELING UPON AWAKENING:
Happy ☐
Sad ☐
Angry ☐
Other: _____

SKETCH YOUR DREAM

Weekly Planner

THURSDAY
☐

FRIDAY
☐

SATURDAY
☐

☐ Things to Do:
☐
☐
☐

SUNDAY
☐

☐ Things to Do:
☐
☐
☐
☐
☐

☐ Things to Do:
☐
☐
☐
☐
☐

*HEAVEN: If you see yourself in heaven, you are living nice moments and have harmony in various aspects of your life. If this is not the case, the dream is telling you to find internal happiness. Read self help books. LN*85141, (1)*

☐ Things to Do:
☐
☐
☐

NOTES

Your Dreams and You Journal & Planner

MONDAY

TUESDAY

WEDNESDAY

_____
_____
_____
_____
_____
_____
_____
_____
_____
_____
_____

☐ Things to Do:
☐ _____
☐ _____
☐ _____
☐ _____
☐ _____
☐ _____

☐ Things to Do:
☐ _____
☐ _____
☐ _____
☐ _____
☐ _____
☐ _____

☐ Things to Do:
☐ _____
☐ _____
☐ _____
☐ _____
☐ _____
☐ _____

FEELING UPON AWAKENING:
Happy ☐
Sad ☐
Angry ☐
Other: _____
_____

SKETCH YOUR DREAM

Weekly Planner

THURSDAY

FRIDAY

SATURDAY

☐ Things to Do:
☐
☐
☐

SUNDAY

☐ Things to Do:
☐ Things to Do:

HOME: It's good luck seeing your own house, especially if it brings you good memories. If it brings you bad memories or it's an empty home, it means family disgrace. LN*8645, (5)

☐ Things to Do:
☐
☐
☐

NOTES

Your Dreams and You Journal & Planner

MONDAY

TUESDAY

WEDNESDAY

☐ Things to Do:
☐
☐
☐
☐
☐
☐

☐ Things to Do:
☐
☐
☐
☐
☐
☐

☐ Things to Do:
☐
☐
☐
☐
☐
☐

FEELING UPON AWAKENING:
Happy ☐
Sad ☐
Angry ☐
Other: _____

SKETCH YOUR DREAM

Weekly Planner

THURSDAY

FRIDAY

SATURDAY

☐ Things to Do:
☐
☐
☐

SUNDAY

☐ Things to Do:

☐ Things to Do:

HUNGER: It's common to be hungry in a dream if you've just started a diet. If not, this isn't a good sign.
LN*83575, (1)

☐ Things to Do:
☐
☐
☐

NOTES

Your Dreams and You Journal & Planner

Month: _____

Monthly Calendar

TO-DO LIST:

NOTES:

This Month's Focus:

| | *Your Dreams and You Journal & Planner* |

MONDAY   TUESDAY   WEDNESDAY

☐ Things to Do: ☐ Things to Do: ☐ Things to Do:

FEELING UPON AWAKENING:
Happy ☐
Sad ☐
Angry ☐
Other: _____

SKETCH YOUR DREAM

Weekly Planner

THURSDAY
☐

FRIDAY
☐

SATURDAY
☐

☐ Things to Do:
☐
☐
☐

SUNDAY
☐

☐ Things to Do:
☐
☐
☐
☐
☐

☐ Things to Do:
☐
☐
☐
☐
☐

☐ Things to Do:
☐
☐
☐

*ISLAND: If you see yourself on an island alone, you'll have difficulties you've created yourself. If you manage to escape, you will resolve the issue. LN*91319, (5)*

NOTES

| 85

Your Dreams and You Journal & Planner

MONDAY

TUESDAY

WEDNESDAY

☐ Things to Do:

☐ Things to Do:

☐ Things to Do:

FEELING UPON AWAKENING:
Happy ☐
Sad ☐
Angry ☐
Other: _____

SKETCH YOUR DREAM

Weekly Planner

THURSDAY

FRIDAY

SATURDAY

☐ Things to Do:
☐
☐
☐

SUNDAY

☐ Things to Do:
☐
☐
☐
☐
☐
☐

☐ Things to Do:
☐
☐
☐
☐
☐
☐

*JEWELS: A favorable sign for those in love, couples, or businesspeople, whether they are gifted to you or you gift them. If someone tries to take them from you, someone wants to rob you. LN*15554, (2)*

☐ Things to Do:
☐
☐
☐

NOTES

Your Dreams and You Journal & Planner

MONDAY	TUESDAY	WEDNESDAY
☐	☐	☐

☐ Things to Do:
☐
☐
☐
☐
☐
☐

☐ Things to Do:
☐
☐
☐
☐
☐
☐

☐ Things to Do:
☐
☐
☐
☐
☐
☐

FEELING UPON AWAKENING:
Happy ☐
Sad ☐
Angry ☐
Other: _____

SKETCH YOUR DREAM

88

Weekly Planner

THURSDAY

FRIDAY

SATURDAY

☐ Things to Do:
☐
☐
☐

SUNDAY

☐ Things to Do:
☐
☐
☐
☐
☐
☐

☐ Things to Do:
☐
☐
☐
☐
☐
☐

*JUMPING: You may experience some obstacles. If you see yourself passing those obstacles, you will be successful in your plans. LN*13473, (9)*

☐ Things to Do:
☐
☐
☐

NOTES

Your Dreams and You Journal & Planner

MONDAY

TUESDAY

WEDNESDAY

☐ Things to Do:

☐ Things to Do:

☐ Things to Do:

FEELING UPON AWAKENING:
Happy ☐
Sad ☐
Angry ☐
Other: _____

SKETCH YOUR DREAM

90 |

Weekly Planner

THURSDAY

FRIDAY

SATURDAY

☐ Things to Do:

SUNDAY

☐ Things to Do:

☐ Things to Do:

☐ Things to Do:

*KNIFE: This has a lot to do with emotions; control yourself. A Broken knife means disappointments. Cutting yourself with a knife means you are losing control of your emotions; calm down. LN*25965, (9)*

NOTES

Your Dreams and You Journal & Planner

MONDAY

TUESDAY

WEDNESDAY

☐ Things to Do:

☐ Things to Do:

☐ Things to Do:

FEELING UPON AWAKENING:
Happy ☐
Sad ☐
Angry ☐
Other: _____

SKETCH YOUR DREAM

Weekly Planner

THURSDAY

FRIDAY

SATURDAY

☐ Things to Do:
☐
☐
☐

SUNDAY

☐ Things to Do:
☐
☐
☐
☐
☐
☐

☐ Things to Do:
☐
☐
☐
☐
☐
☐

*LAKE: If the water is clear and calm, you will enjoy peace and tranquility in your home. If it's murky, it means problems. LN*3125, (11)*

☐ Things to Do:
☐
☐
☐

NOTES

Your Dreams and You Journal & Planner

Month: _____

Monthly Calendar

TO-DO LIST:

NOTES:

This Month's Focus:

Your Dreams and You Journal & Planner

MONDAY

TUESDAY

WEDNESDAY

☐ Things to Do:

☐ Things to Do:

☐ Things to Do:

FEELING UPON AWAKENING:
Happy ☐
Sad ☐
Angry ☐
Other: _____
_____

SKETCH YOUR DREAM

Weekly Planner

THURSDAY

FRIDAY

SATURDAY

☐ Things to Do:
☐
☐
☐

SUNDAY

☐ Things to Do: ☐ Things to Do:
☐ ☐
☐ ☐
☐ ☐
☐ ☐
☐ ☐
☐ ☐

*LION: If you are the lion, it means wisdom and power. If you're attacked or chased by the lion, it means problems with someone you see superior to you. If you're battling with the lion and winning, it means triumph over something it's almost impossible to win. LN*3965, (5)*

☐ Things to Do:
☐
☐
☐

NOTES

Your Dreams and You Journal & Planner

MONDAY

TUESDAY

WEDNESDAY

_____

☐ Things to Do: | ☐ Things to Do: | ☐ Things to Do:

☐
☐
☐
☐
☐
☐

FEELING UPON AWAKENING:
Happy ☐
Sad ☐
Angry ☐
Other: _____
_____

SKETCH YOUR DREAM

Weekly Planner

THURSDAY

FRIDAY

SATURDAY

☐ Things to Do:
☐
☐
☐

SUNDAY

☐ Things to Do:
☐
☐
☐
☐
☐
☐

☐ Things to Do:
☐
☐
☐
☐
☐
☐

*LOVE: It's good if you're not in a relationship. Misery in love is rather good. If it is love amongst friends, this means bliss. LN*3642, (9)*

NOTES

☐ Things to Do:
☐
☐
☐

Your Dreams and You Journal & Planner

MONDAY   TUESDAY   WEDNESDAY

☐ Things to Do: ☐ Things to Do: ☐ Things to Do:

FEELING UPON AWAKENING:
Happy ☐
Sad ☐
Angry ☐
Other: _____
_____

SKETCH YOUR DREAM

Weekly Planner

THURSDAY

FRIDAY

SATURDAY

☐ Things to Do:

SUNDAY

☐ Things to Do:

☐ Things to Do:

*MOON: Feminine intuition, renovation, a hidden side to discover, physical and emotional power of the dreamer. If the moon is beautiful and shining and the sky is clear, happiness in love and bliss. Full moon and clear skies is good for love, as is a new moon for business. LN*4665, (21)*

☐ Things to Do:

NOTES

Your Dreams and You Journal & Planner

MONDAY ☐	TUESDAY ☐	WEDNESDAY ☐
_____	_____	_____

☐ Things to Do: | ☐ Things to Do: | ☐ Things to Do:
☐
☐
☐
☐
☐
☐

FEELING UPON AWAKENING:
Happy ☐
Sad ☐
Angry ☐
Other: _____

SKETCH YOUR DREAM

Weekly Planner

THURSDAY
☐

FRIDAY
☐

SATURDAY
☐

☐ Things to Do:
☐
☐
☐

SUNDAY
☐

☐ Things to Do:
☐
☐
☐
☐
☐
☐

☐ Things to Do:
☐
☐
☐
☐
☐
☐

NEST: It's excellent for your business if there are eggs or hatchlings. If the nest is empty, you have a long way to go for your project. If someone destroys it or eats the babies, it means big losses. LN*5512, (4)

☐ Things to Do:
☐
☐
☐

NOTES

Your Dreams and You Journal & Planner

MONDAY

TUESDAY

WEDNESDAY

☐ Things to Do: ☐ Things to Do: ☐ Things to Do:

FEELING UPON AWAKENING:
Happy ☐
Sad ☐
Angry ☐
Other: _____

SKETCH YOUR DREAM

Weekly Planner

THURSDAY

FRIDAY

SATURDAY

☐ Things to Do:

SUNDAY

☐ Things to Do:

☐ Things to Do:

☐ Things to Do:

*NUDITY: The less clothes you have on the better. It means better financial status, sensuality, and fulfillment of desires. Not being embarrassed in doing anything in life, accepting oneself. LN*53499, (3)*

NOTES

Your Dreams and You Journal & Planner

Month: _____

Monthly Calendar

TO-DO LIST:

NOTES:

This Month's Focus:

Your Dreams and You Journal & Planner

MONDAY TUESDAY WEDNESDAY

☐ Things to Do: ☐ Things to Do: ☐ Things to Do:

FEELING UPON AWAKENING:
Happy ☐
Sad ☐
Angry ☐
Other: _____
_____

SKETCH YOUR DREAM

Weekly Planner

THURSDAY

FRIDAY

SATURDAY

☐ Things to Do:
☐
☐
☐

SUNDAY

☐ Things to Do:
☐
☐
☐
☐
☐
☐

☐ Things to Do:
☐
☐
☐
☐
☐
☐

*OBSTACLE: This is a warning dream of difficulties. If you beat the obstacles, this is a good sign. Look for help to overcome the obstacle. LN*62124, (6)*

☐ Things to Do:
☐
☐
☐

NOTES

Your Dreams and You Journal & Planner

MONDAY

TUESDAY

WEDNESDAY

☐ Things to Do:

☐ Things to Do:

☐ Things to Do:

FEELING UPON AWAKENING:
Happy ☐
Sad ☐
Angry ☐
Other: _____

SKETCH YOUR DREAM

Weekly Planner

THURSDAY

☐

FRIDAY

☐

SATURDAY

☐

☐ Things to Do:
☐
☐
☐

SUNDAY

☐

☐ Things to Do: ☐ Things to Do:
☐   ☐
☐   ☐
☐   ☐
☐   ☐
☐   ☐
☐   ☐

*OLD PERSON: To see the elderly is one of the wisest dreams there is. It reflects maturity in the dreamer and the culmination of a project. LN*63477, (9)*

☐ Things to Do:
☐
☐
☐

NOTES

Your Dreams and You Journal & Planner

MONDAY

TUESDAY

WEDNESDAY

☐ Things to Do:

☐ Things to Do:

☐ Things to Do:

FEELING UPON AWAKENING:
Happy ☐
Sad ☐
Angry ☐
Other: _____

SKETCH YOUR DREAM

Weekly Planner

THURSDAY
☐

FRIDAY
☐

SATURDAY
☐

☐ Things to Do:
☐
☐
☐

SUNDAY
☐

☐ Things to Do:
☐
☐
☐
☐
☐
☐

☐ Things to Do:
☐
☐
☐
☐
☐
☐

*PARENTS: You must solve past problems. If they are distanced from you physically, connect more with them. LN*71958, (3)*

☐ Things to Do:
☐
☐
☐

NOTES

Your Dreams and You Journal & Planner

MONDAY

TUESDAY

WEDNESDAY

☐ Things to Do:

☐ Things to Do:

☐ Things to Do:

FEELING UPON AWAKENING:
Happy ☐
Sad ☐
Angry ☐
Other: _____

SKETCH YOUR DREAM

114 |

Weekly Planner

THURSDAY
☐

FRIDAY
☐

SATURDAY
☐

☐ Things to Do:
☐
☐
☐

SUNDAY
☐

☐ Things to Do:
☐
☐
☐
☐
☐

☐ Things to Do:
☐
☐
☐
☐
☐

*PARTNER: If you see your partner kiss someone else, as long as you don't know them, don't worry. If the dream is recurrent regarding your partner, analyze your behavior. LN*71921, (2)*

☐ Things to Do:
☐
☐
☐

NOTES

Your Dreams and You Journal & Planner

MONDAY

TUESDAY

WEDNESDAY

☐ Things to Do:
☐
☐
☐
☐
☐
☐

☐ Things to Do:
☐
☐
☐
☐
☐
☐

☐ Things to Do:
☐
☐
☐
☐
☐
☐

FEELING UPON AWAKENING:
Happy ☐
Sad ☐
Angry ☐
Other: _____
_____

SKETCH YOUR DREAM

Weekly Planner

THURSDAY

FRIDAY

SATURDAY

☐ Things to Do:

SUNDAY

☐ Things to Do:

☐ Things to Do:

☐ Things to Do:

PAIN: Reflects regret of the dreamer, something the dreamer may have done consciously or unconsciously. If the pain is soft, it is related to health. If the pain is deep, possible financial gains as long as the dreamer has not done anything to anyone recently. LN*7195, (5)

NOTES

Month: _____

Monthly Calendar

TO-DO LIST:

NOTES:

This Month's Focus:

Your Dreams and You Journal & Planner

☐ MONDAY ☐	TUESDAY ☐	WEDNESDAY ☐
☐ Things to Do:	☐ Things to Do:	☐ Things to Do:

FEELING UPON AWAKENING:
Happy ☐
Sad ☐
Angry ☐
Other: _____

SKETCH YOUR DREAM

120 |

Weekly Planner

THURSDAY

FRIDAY

SATURDAY

☐ Things to Do:
☐
☐
☐

SUNDAY

☐ Things to Do: ☐ Things to Do:
☐   ☐
☐   ☐
☐   ☐
☐   ☐
☐   ☐

*RAINBOW: An excellent dream, you have or will have good fortune in love, matrimony or family. LN*91954, (1)*

☐ Things to Do:
☐
☐
☐

NOTES

Your Dreams and You Journal & Planner

MONDAY

TUESDAY

WEDNESDAY

☐ Things to Do:
☐
☐
☐
☐
☐
☐

☐ Things to Do:
☐
☐
☐
☐
☐
☐

☐ Things to Do:
☐
☐
☐
☐
☐
☐

FEELING UPON AWAKENING:
Happy ☐
Sad ☐
Angry ☐
Other: _____
_____

SKETCH YOUR DREAM

Weekly Planner

THURSDAY
☐

FRIDAY
☐

SATURDAY
☐

☐ Things to Do:
☐
☐
☐

SUNDAY
☐

☐ Things to Do:
☐
☐
☐
☐
☐
☐

☐ Things to Do:
☐
☐
☐
☐
☐
☐

*RIVER: If you swim against the current and can't get to where you want, you can't go against the problem. The best is to tackle the problem even if you don't like it. If you go with the current, that is your life, in favor. LN*99459, (8)*

☐ Things to Do:
☐
☐
☐

NOTES

Your Dreams and You Journal & Planner

MONDAY

TUESDAY

WEDNESDAY

☐ Things to Do:
☐
☐
☐
☐
☐
☐

☐ Things to Do:
☐
☐
☐
☐
☐
☐

☐ Things to Do:
☐
☐
☐
☐
☐
☐

FEELING UPON AWAKENING:
Happy ☐
Sad ☐
Angry ☐
Other: _____
_____

SKETCH YOUR DREAM

Weekly Planner

THURSDAY

FRIDAY

SATURDAY

☐ Things to Do:

SUNDAY

☐ Things to Do:

☐ Things to Do:

SCHOOL: Being in school shows stress in the dreamer or childhood memories. If you are in school, you have worries. These can also mean new projects for businesspeople. LN*13869, (9)

☐ Things to Do:

NOTES

Your Dreams and You Journal & Planner

MONDAY

TUESDAY

WEDNESDAY

Things to Do:

Things to Do:

Things to Do:

FEELING UPON AWAKENING:
Happy
Sad
Angry
Other: _____

SKETCH YOUR DREAM

Weekly Planner

THURSDAY

FRIDAY

SATURDAY

☐ Things to Do:
☐
☐
☐

SUNDAY

☐ Things to Do:
☐ Things to Do:

☐ Things to Do:
☐
☐
☐

*SELLING: If you sell at a higher price, it means success in business. If you sell at a lower price, you'll have financial struggles. Be careful with your expenses. LN*15393, (21)*

NOTES

Your Dreams and You Journal & Planner

MONDAY

TUESDAY

WEDNESDAY

☐ Things to Do:

☐ Things to Do:

☐ Things to Do:

FEELING UPON AWAKENING:
Happy ☐
Sad ☐
Angry ☐
Other: _____

SKETCH YOUR DREAM

Weekly Planner

THURSDAY
☐

FRIDAY
☐

SATURDAY
☐

☐ Things to Do:
☐
☐
☐

SUNDAY
☐

☐ Things to Do:
☐
☐
☐
☐
☐
☐

☐ Things to Do:
☐
☐
☐
☐
☐

☐ Things to Do:
☐
☐
☐

*SHOES: New shoes mean new projects with good alternatives; if they're clean it means success; dirty shoes mean illnesses, conflicts; broken shoes mean financial imbalance, poverty; barefoot means submission or success. LN*18651, (21)*

NOTES

Month: _____

Monthly Calendar

TO-DO LIST:

NOTES:

This Month's Focus:

Your Dreams and You Journal & Planner

MONDAY	TUESDAY	WEDNESDAY
☐	☐	☐

☐ Things to Do: ☐ Things to Do: ☐ Things to Do:

FEELING UPON AWAKENING:
Happy ☐
Sad ☐
Angry ☐
Other: _____
_____

SKETCH YOUR DREAM

Weekly Planner

THURSDAY

FRIDAY

SATURDAY

☐ Things to Do:

SUNDAY

☐ Things to Do:

☐ Things to Do:

☐ Things to Do:

*SNOW: Because of its whiteness and purity it is associated with honor and security. Snow in your house or business means abundance. LN*1565, (8)*

NOTES

Your Dreams and You Journal & Planner

MONDAY

TUESDAY

WEDNESDAY

☐ Things to Do:

☐ Things to Do:

☐ Things to Do:

FEELING UPON AWAKENING:
Happy ☐
Sad ☐
Angry ☐
Other: _____

SKETCH YOUR DREAM

Weekly Planner

THURSDAY

FRIDAY

SATURDAY

☐ Things to Do:

SUNDAY

☐ Things to Do:

☐ Things to Do:

STRANGERS: As long as you have good relations with strangers there is no problem. If you are facing a problem, you will resolve anything that comes your way. LN*12919, (4)

☐ Things to Do:

NOTES

Your Dreams and You Journal & Planner

MONDAY

TUESDAY

WEDNESDAY

☐ Things to Do:

☐ Things to Do:

☐ Things to Do:

FEELING UPON AWAKENING:
Happy ☐
Sad ☐
Angry ☐
Other: _____
_____

SKETCH YOUR DREAM

Weekly Planner

THURSDAY

FRIDAY

SATURDAY

☐ Things to Do:

SUNDAY

☐ Things to Do:

☐ Things to Do:

☐ Things to Do:

*TALKING: If you know what you are talking about and it has a meaning, it shows the power of speech. If you don't understand what you're saying or are afraid of expressing yourself freely, beware of slander. LN*21323, (2)*

NOTES

Your Dreams and You Journal & Planner

MONDAY ☐	TUESDAY ☐	WEDNESDAY ☐
_____	_____	_____
_____	_____	_____
_____	_____	_____
_____	_____	_____
_____	_____	_____
_____	_____	_____
_____	_____	_____
_____	_____	_____
_____	_____	_____
_____	_____	_____

☐ Things to Do:
☐
☐
☐
☐
☐
☐

☐ Things to Do:
☐
☐
☐
☐
☐
☐

☐ Things to Do:
☐
☐
☐
☐
☐
☐

FEELING UPON AWAKENING:
Happy ☐
Sad ☐
Angry ☐
Other: _____

SKETCH YOUR DREAM

Weekly Planner

THURSDAY

FRIDAY

SATURDAY

☐ Things to Do:

SUNDAY

☐ Things to Do:

☐ Things to Do:

☐ Things to Do:

*THIEF: Warns of distrust towards others, a warning to revise everything at home or business. If you catch the thief, you'll be successful. If you see them and don't catch them and it's night time or dark, you'll have problems. LN*28956, (3)*

NOTES

Your Dreams and You Journal & Planner

MONDAY

TUESDAY

WEDNESDAY

☐ Things to Do:

☐ Things to Do:

☐ Things to Do:

FEELING UPON AWAKENING:
Happy ☐
Sad ☐
Angry ☐
Other: _____

SKETCH YOUR DREAM

Weekly Planner

THURSDAY

FRIDAY

SATURDAY

☐ Things to Do:

SUNDAY

☐ Things to Do:

☐ Things to Do:

*TRAIN: Points to changes in your life. If the journey is pleasant, your path will be positive. If it's a short trip, you'll be far away from your family. Traveling with your family is family reunification. LN*29195, (8)*

☐ Things to Do:

NOTES

Month: _____

Monthly Calendar

TO-DO LIST:

NOTES:

This Month's Focus:

Your Dreams and You Journal & Planner

MONDAY	TUESDAY	WEDNESDAY

☐ Things to Do:

☐ Things to Do:

☐ Things to Do:

FEELING UPON AWAKENING:
Happy ☐
Sad ☐
Angry ☐
Other: _____

SKETCH YOUR DREAM

Weekly Planner

THURSDAY

FRIDAY

SATURDAY

☐ Things to Do:

SUNDAY

☐ Things to Do:

☐ Things to Do:

☐ Things to Do:

UNIVERSE: Success. If fire or meteorites fall from the universe, it means catastrophe. The way you sound and feel when you wake up is important for the interpretation. If you feel good and it's positive, unlimited wealth. LN*354515, (12)

NOTES

Your Dreams and You Journal & Planner

MONDAY

TUESDAY

WEDNESDAY

☐ Things to Do:
☐
☐
☐
☐
☐
☐

☐ Things to Do:
☐
☐
☐
☐
☐
☐

☐ Things to Do:
☐
☐
☐
☐
☐
☐

FEELING UPON AWAKENING:
Happy ☐
Sad ☐
Angry ☐
Other: _____
_____

SKETCH YOUR DREAM

Weekly Planner

THURSDAY ☐

FRIDAY ☐

SATURDAY ☐

☐ Things to Do:
☐
☐
☐

SUNDAY ☐

☐ Things to Do:
☐
☐
☐
☐
☐

☐ Things to Do:
☐
☐
☐
☐
☐

*WALKING: If you're walking in the daylight, this is a good sign. Walking on water means definite success. LN*513257, (5)*

NOTES

☐ Things to Do:
☐
☐
☐

Your Dreams and You Journal & Planner

MONDAY

TUESDAY

WEDNESDAY

☐ Things to Do:

☐ Things to Do:

☐ Things to Do:

FEELING UPON AWAKENING:
Happy ☐
Sad ☐
Angry ☐
Other: _____
_____

SKETCH YOUR DREAM

Weekly Planner

THURSDAY
FRIDAY
SATURDAY

☐ Things to Do:

SUNDAY

☐ Things to Do: ☐ Things to Do:

WISE: Dreaming about a wise person represents your need to not only learn and receive information but also advice. You may be going through a tough situation, and you'll have to make wise decisions. Look for informed people so you can make an informed decision. LN*5915, (2)

☐ Things to Do:

NOTES

Your Dreams and You Journal & Planner

MONDAY	TUESDAY	WEDNESDAY

☐ Things to Do: ☐ Things to Do: ☐ Things to Do:

FEELING UPON AWAKENING:
Happy ☐
Sad ☐
Angry ☐
Other: _____
_____

SKETCH YOUR DREAM

Weekly Planner

THURSDAY
☐

FRIDAY
☐

SATURDAY
☐

☐ Things to Do:
☐
☐
☐

SUNDAY
☐

☐ Things to Do:
☐
☐
☐
☐
☐

☐ Things to Do:
☐
☐
☐
☐
☐

☐ Things to Do:
☐
☐
☐

*YELLOW: The color yellow represents mental qualities and power, the color of the sun (gold). If it is dark yellow, low passions. Light yellow, material stability. LN*753365, (2)*

NOTES

Your Dreams and You Journal & Planner

MONDAY

TUESDAY

WEDNESDAY

☐ Things to Do:

☐ Things to Do:

☐ Things to Do:

FEELING UPON AWAKENING:
Happy ☐
Sad ☐
Angry ☐
Other: _____
_____

SKETCH YOUR DREAM

Weekly Planner

THURSDAY

FRIDAY

SATURDAY

☐ Things to Do:
☐
☐
☐

SUNDAY

☐ Things to Do:
☐
☐
☐
☐
☐
☐

☐ Things to Do:
☐
☐
☐
☐
☐
☐

*ZEBRA: Good and bad. You're going through moments in your life in which you don't know the right decision to make, especially if it's related to choosing a partner. LN*85291, (7)*

☐ Things to Do:
☐
☐
☐

NOTES

Your Dreams and You Journal & Planner

Date: _____ Time: _____

Possible timeframe: ☐ Past ☐ Present ☐ Future ☐ Unknown

Feeling & Description: ☐ Happy ☐ Sad ☐ Anger
☐ Other _____

Location: _____

People: _____

Objects and Things: _____

Colors: _____

Numbers: _____

Animals: _____

Actions: _____

Describe the Dream:

_____
_____
_____
_____
_____
_____
_____
_____
_____
_____
_____
_____

Dream Journal

Draw Your Dream:

Dream Meaning:

_____
_____
_____
_____
_____
_____
_____

Notes:

_____
_____
_____
_____
_____
_____
_____
_____

Date: _____ Time: _____

Possible timeframe: ☐ Past ☐ Present ☐ Future ☐ Unknown

Feeling & Description: ☐ Happy ☐ Sad ☐ Anger

☐ Other _____

Location: _____

People: _____

Objects and Things: _____

Colors: _____

Numbers: _____

Animals: _____

Actions: _____

Describe the Dream:

_____
_____
_____
_____
_____
_____
_____
_____
_____
_____
_____

Dream Journal

Draw Your Dream:

Dream Meaning:

_____
_____
_____
_____
_____
_____

Notes:

_____
_____
_____
_____
_____
_____
_____

Date: _____ Time: _____

Possible timeframe: ☐ Past ☐ Present ☐ Future ☐ Unknown

Feeling & Description: ☐ Happy ☐ Sad ☐ Anger

☐ Other _____

Location: _____

People: _____

Objects and Things: _____

Colors: _____

Numbers: _____

Animals: _____

Actions: _____

Describe the Dream:

_____
_____
_____
_____
_____
_____
_____
_____
_____
_____
_____
_____
_____

Dream Journal

Draw Your Dream:

Dream Meaning:

_____
_____
_____
_____
_____
_____
_____

Notes:

_____
_____
_____
_____
_____
_____
_____
_____

Your Dreams and You Journal & Planner

Date: _____ Time: _____

Possible timeframe: ☐ Past ☐ Present ☐ Future ☐ Unknown

Feeling & Description: ☐ Happy ☐ Sad ☐ Anger

☐ Other _____

Location: _____

People: _____

Objects and Things: _____

Colors: _____

Numbers: _____

Animals: _____

Actions: _____

Describe the Dream:

_____
_____
_____
_____
_____
_____
_____
_____
_____
_____
_____

Dream Journal

Draw Your Dream:

Dream Meaning:

_____
_____
_____
_____
_____
_____
_____

Notes:

_____
_____
_____
_____
_____
_____
_____

Your Dreams and You Journal & Planner

Date: ☐   Time: ☐

Possible timeframe: ☐ Past ☐ Present ☐ Future ☐ Unknown

Feeling & Description: ☐ Happy ☐ Sad ☐ Anger

☐ Other _____

Location: _____

People: _____

Objects and Things: _____

Colors: _____

Numbers: _____

Animals: _____

Actions: _____

Describe the Dream:

_____
_____
_____
_____
_____
_____
_____
_____
_____
_____
_____
_____

Dream Journal

Draw Your Dream:

Dream Meaning:

_____
_____
_____
_____
_____
_____

Notes:

_____
_____
_____
_____
_____
_____
_____
_____

Date: _____ Time: _____

Possible timeframe: ☐ Past ☐ Present ☐ Future ☐ Unknown

Feeling & Description: ☐ Happy ☐ Sad ☐ Anger

☐ Other _____

Location: _____

People: _____

Objects and Things: _____

Colors: _____

Numbers: _____

Animals: _____

Actions: _____

Describe the Dream:

_____
_____
_____
_____
_____
_____
_____
_____
_____
_____
_____
_____

Dream Journal

Draw Your Dream:

Dream Meaning:

_____
_____
_____
_____
_____
_____
_____

Notes:

_____
_____
_____
_____
_____
_____
_____
_____

Date: _____ Time: _____

Possible timeframe: ☐ Past ☐ Present ☐ Future ☐ Unknown

Feeling & Description: ☐ Happy ☐ Sad ☐ Anger

☐ Other _____

Location: _____

People: _____

Objects and Things: _____

Colors: _____

Numbers: _____

Animals: _____

Actions: _____

Describe the Dream:

_____
_____
_____
_____
_____
_____
_____
_____
_____
_____
_____
_____

Dream Journal

Draw Your Dream:

Dream Meaning:

_____
_____
_____
_____
_____
_____
_____

Notes:

_____
_____
_____
_____
_____
_____
_____
_____

Date: _____ Time: _____

Possible timeframe: ☐ Past ☐ Present ☐ Future ☐ Unknown

Feeling & Description: ☐ Happy ☐ Sad ☐ Anger
☐ Other _____

Location: _____

People: _____

Objects and Things: _____

Colors: _____

Numbers: _____

Animals: _____

Actions: _____

Describe the Dream:

_____
_____
_____
_____
_____
_____
_____
_____
_____
_____
_____
_____
_____
_____

Dream Journal

Draw Your Dream:

Dream Meaning:

_____
_____
_____
_____
_____
_____
_____

Notes:

_____
_____
_____
_____
_____
_____
_____

Your Dreams and You Journal & Planner

Date: _____ Time: _____

Possible timeframe: ☐ Past ☐ Present ☐ Future ☐ Unknown

Feeling & Description: ☐ Happy ☐ Sad ☐ Anger

☐ Other _____

Location: _____

People: _____

Objects and Things: _____

Colors: _____

Numbers: _____

Animals: _____

Actions: _____

Describe the Dream:

_____

_____

_____

_____

_____

_____

_____

_____

_____

_____

_____

_____

Dream Journal

Draw Your Dream:

Dream Meaning:

Notes:

Your Dreams and You Journal & Planner

Date: ☐　　　　　　　　Time: ☐

Possible timeframe: ☐ Past　☐ Present　☐ Future　☐ Unknown

Feeling & Description: ☐ Happy　☐ Sad　☐ Anger
☐ Other _____

Location: _____

People: _____

Objects and Things: _____

Colors: _____

Numbers: _____

Animals: _____

Actions: _____

Describe the Dream:

_____
_____
_____
_____
_____
_____
_____
_____
_____
_____

Dream Journal

Draw Your Dream:

Dream Meaning:

Notes:

Your Dreams and You Journal & Planner

Date: ☐ Time: ☐
Possible timeframe: ☐ Past ☐ Present ☐ Future ☐ Unknown
Feeling & Description: ☐ Happy ☐ Sad ☐ Anger
☐ Other _____

Location: _____
People: _____
Objects and Things: _____
Colors: _____
Numbers: _____
Animals: _____
Actions: _____
Describe the Dream:
_____
_____
_____
_____
_____
_____
_____
_____
_____
_____
_____

Dream Journal

Draw Your Dream:

Dream Meaning:

Notes:

Your Dreams and You Journal & Planner

Date: _____ Time: _____

Possible timeframe: ☐ Past ☐ Present ☐ Future ☐ Unknown

Feeling & Description: ☐ Happy ☐ Sad ☐ Anger

☐ Other _____

Location: _____

People: _____

Objects and Things: _____

Colors: _____

Numbers: _____

Animals: _____

Actions: _____

Describe the Dream:

_____
_____
_____
_____
_____
_____
_____
_____
_____
_____
_____
_____
_____

Dream Journal

Draw Your Dream:

Dream Meaning:

_____
_____
_____
_____
_____
_____

Notes:

_____
_____
_____
_____
_____
_____
_____
_____

Your Dreams and You Journal & Planner

Date: _____ Time: _____

Possible timeframe: ☐ Past ☐ Present ☐ Future ☐ Unknown

Feeling & Description: ☐ Happy ☐ Sad ☐ Anger
☐ Other _____

Location: _____

People: _____

Objects and Things: _____

Colors: _____

Numbers: _____

Animals: _____

Actions: _____

Describe the Dream:

_____
_____
_____
_____
_____
_____
_____
_____
_____
_____
_____
_____

Dream Journal

Draw Your Dream:

Dream Meaning:

_____
_____
_____
_____
_____
_____
_____

Notes:

_____
_____
_____
_____
_____
_____
_____
_____

Date: _____ Time: _____

Possible timeframe: ☐ Past ☐ Present ☐ Future ☐ Unknown

Feeling & Description: ☐ Happy ☐ Sad ☐ Anger

☐ Other _____

Location: _____

People: _____

Objects and Things: _____

Colors: _____

Numbers: _____

Animals: _____

Actions: _____

Describe the Dream:

_____

_____

_____

_____

_____

_____

_____

_____

_____

_____

_____

Dream Journal

Draw Your Dream:

Dream Meaning:

_____
_____
_____
_____
_____
_____
_____

Notes:

_____
_____
_____
_____
_____
_____
_____

Date: _____ Time: _____

Possible timeframe: ☐ Past ☐ Present ☐ Future ☐ Unknown

Feeling & Description: ☐ Happy ☐ Sad ☐ Anger

☐ Other _____

Location: _____

People: _____

Objects and Things: _____

Colors: _____

Numbers: _____

Animals: _____

Actions: _____

Describe the Dream:

_____
_____
_____
_____
_____
_____
_____
_____
_____
_____
_____
_____

Dream Journal

Draw Your Dream:

Dream Meaning:

_____
_____
_____
_____
_____
_____
_____

Notes:

_____
_____
_____
_____
_____
_____
_____
_____

Your Dreams and You Journal & Planner

Date: _____ Time: _____

Possible timeframe: ☐ Past ☐ Present ☐ Future ☐ Unknown

Feeling & Description: ☐ Happy ☐ Sad ☐ Anger
☐ Other _____

Location: _____

People: _____

Objects and Things: _____

Colors: _____

Numbers: _____

Animals: _____

Actions: _____

Describe the Dream:

_____
_____
_____
_____
_____
_____
_____
_____
_____
_____
_____

Dream Journal

Draw Your Dream:

Dream Meaning:

Notes:

Your Dreams and You Journal & Planner

Date: _____   Time: _____

Possible timeframe: ☐ Past ☐ Present ☐ Future ☐ Unknown

Feeling & Description: ☐ Happy ☐ Sad ☐ Anger
☐ Other _____

Location: _____

People: _____

Objects and Things: _____

Colors: _____

Numbers: _____

Animals: _____

Actions: _____

Describe the Dream:

_____
_____
_____
_____
_____
_____
_____
_____
_____
_____
_____

Dream Journal

Draw Your Dream:

Dream Meaning:

___
___
___
___
___
___

Notes:

___
___
___
___
___
___
___

Date: _____ Time: _____

Possible timeframe: ☐ Past ☐ Present ☐ Future ☐ Unknown

Feeling & Description: ☐ Happy ☐ Sad ☐ Anger

☐ Other _____

Location: _____

People: _____

Objects and Things: _____

Colors: _____

Numbers: _____

Animals: _____

Actions: _____

Describe the Dream:

_____
_____
_____
_____
_____
_____
_____
_____
_____
_____
_____
_____

Dream Journal

Draw Your Dream:

Dream Meaning:

Notes:

Your Dreams and You Journal & Planner

Date: _____ Time: _____

Possible timeframe: ☐ Past ☐ Present ☐ Future ☐ Unknown

Feeling & Description: ☐ Happy ☐ Sad ☐ Anger
☐ Other _____

Location: _____

People: _____

Objects and Things: _____

Colors: _____

Numbers: _____

Animals: _____

Actions: _____

Describe the Dream:

_____
_____
_____
_____
_____
_____
_____
_____
_____
_____
_____

Dream Journal

Draw Your Dream:

Dream Meaning:

Notes:

Your Dreams and You Journal & Planner

Date: _____ Time: _____

Possible timeframe: ☐ Past ☐ Present ☐ Future ☐ Unknown

Feeling & Description: ☐ Happy ☐ Sad ☐ Anger
☐ Other _____

Location: _____

People: _____

Objects and Things: _____

Colors: _____

Numbers: _____

Animals: _____

Actions: _____

Describe the Dream:

_____
_____
_____
_____
_____
_____
_____
_____
_____
_____
_____
_____
_____

Dream Journal

Draw Your Dream:

Dream Meaning:

_____
_____
_____
_____
_____
_____

Notes:

_____
_____
_____
_____
_____
_____
_____

Your Dreams and You Journal & Planner

Date: _____ Time: _____

Possible timeframe: ☐ Past ☐ Present ☐ Future ☐ Unknown

Feeling & Description: ☐ Happy ☐ Sad ☐ Anger

☐ Other _____

Location: _____

People: _____

Objects and Things: _____

Colors: _____

Numbers: _____

Animals: _____

Actions: _____

Describe the Dream:

_____
_____
_____
_____
_____
_____
_____
_____
_____
_____
_____
_____
_____

Dream Journal

Draw Your Dream:

Dream Meaning:

_____
_____
_____
_____
_____
_____
_____

Notes:

_____
_____
_____
_____
_____
_____
_____
_____

Date: _____   Time: _____

Possible timeframe: ☐ Past ☐ Present ☐ Future ☐ Unknown

Feeling & Description: ☐ Happy ☐ Sad ☐ Anger

☐ Other _____

Location: _____

People: _____

Objects and Things: _____

Colors: _____

Numbers: _____

Animals: _____

Actions: _____

Describe the Dream:

_____
_____
_____
_____
_____
_____
_____
_____
_____
_____
_____

Dream Journal

Draw Your Dream:

Dream Meaning:

_____
_____
_____
_____
_____
_____
_____

Notes:

_____
_____
_____
_____
_____
_____
_____
_____

Your Dreams and You Journal & Planner

Date: _____ Time: _____

Possible timeframe: ☐ Past ☐ Present ☐ Future ☐ Unknown

Feeling & Description: ☐ Happy ☐ Sad ☐ Anger

☐ Other _____

Location: _____

People: _____

Objects and Things: _____

Colors: _____

Numbers: _____

Animals: _____

Actions: _____

Describe the Dream:

_____
_____
_____
_____
_____
_____
_____
_____
_____
_____
_____
_____

Dream Journal

Draw Your Dream:

Dream Meaning:

___

___

___

___

___

___

___

Notes:

___

___

___

___

___

___

___

___

Your Dreams and You Journal & Planner

Date: _____ Time: _____

Possible timeframe: ☐ Past ☐ Present ☐ Future ☐ Unknown

Feeling & Description: ☐ Happy ☐ Sad ☐ Anger
☐ Other _____

Location: _____

People: _____

Objects and Things: _____

Colors: _____

Numbers: _____

Animals: _____

Actions: _____

Describe the Dream:

_____
_____
_____
_____
_____
_____
_____
_____
_____
_____
_____
_____
_____

Dream Journal

Draw Your Dream:

Dream Meaning:

Notes:

Date: _____ Time: _____

Possible timeframe: ☐ Past ☐ Present ☐ Future ☐ Unknown

Feeling & Description: ☐ Happy ☐ Sad ☐ Anger
☐ Other _____

Location: _____

People: _____

Objects and Things: _____

Colors: _____

Numbers: _____

Animals: _____

Actions: _____

Describe the Dream:

_____
_____
_____
_____
_____
_____
_____
_____
_____
_____
_____
_____

Dream Journal

Draw Your Dream:

Dream Meaning:

Notes:

Date: _____ Time: _____

Possible timeframe: ☐ Past ☐ Present ☐ Future ☐ Unknown

Feeling & Description: ☐ Happy ☐ Sad ☐ Anger

☐ Other _____

Location: _____

People: _____

Objects and Things: _____

Colors: _____

Numbers: _____

Animals: _____

Actions: _____

Describe the Dream:

_____
_____
_____
_____
_____
_____
_____
_____
_____
_____
_____
_____

Dream Journal

Draw Your Dream:

Dream Meaning:

Notes:

Your Dreams and You Journal & Planner

Date: _____ Time: _____

Possible timeframe: ☐ Past ☐ Present ☐ Future ☐ Unknown

Feeling & Description: ☐ Happy ☐ Sad ☐ Anger

☐ Other _____

Location: _____

People: _____

Objects and Things: _____

Colors: _____

Numbers: _____

Animals: _____

Actions: _____

Describe the Dream:

_____
_____
_____
_____
_____
_____
_____
_____
_____
_____
_____

Dream Journal

Draw Your Dream:

Dream Meaning:

Notes:

Date: _____ Time: _____

Possible timeframe: ☐ Past ☐ Present ☐ Future ☐ Unknown

Feeling & Description: ☐ Happy ☐ Sad ☐ Anger

☐ Other _____

Location: _____

People: _____

Objects and Things: _____

Colors: _____

Numbers: _____

Animals: _____

Actions: _____

Describe the Dream:

_____

_____

_____

_____

_____

_____

_____

_____

_____

_____

_____

_____

Dream Journal

Draw Your Dream:

Dream Meaning:

Notes:

Your Dreams and You Journal & Planner

Date: _____ Time: _____

Possible timeframe: ☐ Past ☐ Present ☐ Future ☐ Unknown

Feeling & Description: ☐ Happy ☐ Sad ☐ Anger

☐ Other _____

Location: _____

People: _____

Objects and Things: _____

Colors: _____

Numbers: _____

Animals: _____

Actions: _____

Describe the Dream:

_____
_____
_____
_____
_____
_____
_____
_____
_____
_____
_____

Dream Journal

Draw Your Dream:

Dream Meaning:

Notes:

Your Dreams and You Journal & Planner

Date: _____ Time: _____

Possible timeframe: ☐ Past ☐ Present ☐ Future ☐ Unknown

Feeling & Description: ☐ Happy ☐ Sad ☐ Anger

☐ Other _____

Location: _____

People: _____

Objects and Things: _____

Colors: _____

Numbers: _____

Animals: _____

Actions: _____

Describe the Dream:

_____
_____
_____
_____
_____
_____
_____
_____
_____
_____
_____
_____

Dream Journal

Draw Your Dream:

Dream Meaning:

_____
_____
_____
_____
_____
_____
_____

Notes:

_____
_____
_____
_____
_____
_____
_____

Your Dreams and You Journal & Planner

Date: _____ Time: _____

Possible timeframe: ☐ Past ☐ Present ☐ Future ☐ Unknown

Feeling & Description: ☐ Happy ☐ Sad ☐ Anger
☐ Other _____

Location: _____

People: _____

Objects and Things: _____

Colors: _____

Numbers: _____

Animals: _____

Actions: _____

Describe the Dream:

_____
_____
_____
_____
_____
_____
_____
_____
_____
_____
_____
_____

Dream Journal

Draw Your Dream:

Dream Meaning:

Notes:

Date: _____ *Time:* _____

Possible timeframe: ☐ *Past* ☐ *Present* ☐ *Future* ☐ *Unknown*

Feeling & Description: ☐ *Happy* ☐ *Sad* ☐ *Anger*

☐ *Other* _____

Location: _____

People: _____

Objects and Things: _____

Colors: _____

Numbers: _____

Animals: _____

Actions: _____

Describe the Dream:

_____
_____
_____
_____
_____
_____
_____
_____
_____
_____
_____

Dream Journal

Draw Your Dream:

Dream Meaning:

_____
_____
_____
_____
_____
_____

Notes:

_____
_____
_____
_____
_____
_____
_____

Date: _____ Time: _____

Possible timeframe: ☐ Past ☐ Present ☐ Future ☐ Unknown

Feeling & Description: ☐ Happy ☐ Sad ☐ Anger

☐ Other _____

Location: _____

People: _____

Objects and Things: _____

Colors: _____

Numbers: _____

Animals: _____

Actions: _____

Describe the Dream:

_____
_____
_____
_____
_____
_____
_____
_____
_____
_____
_____
_____

Dream Journal

Draw Your Dream:

Dream Meaning:

Notes:

Your Dreams and You Journal & Planner

Date: _____ Time: _____

Possible timeframe: ☐ Past ☐ Present ☐ Future ☐ Unknown

Feeling & Description: ☐ Happy ☐ Sad ☐ Anger
☐ Other _____

Location: _____

People: _____

Objects and Things: _____

Colors: _____

Numbers: _____

Animals: _____

Actions: _____

Describe the Dream:

_____
_____
_____
_____
_____
_____
_____
_____
_____
_____
_____
_____

Dream Journal

Draw Your Dream:

Dream Meaning:

_____
_____
_____
_____
_____
_____
_____

Notes:

_____
_____
_____
_____
_____
_____
_____

Date: _____ Time: _____

Possible timeframe: ☐ Past ☐ Present ☐ Future ☐ Unknown

Feeling & Description: ☐ Happy ☐ Sad ☐ Anger
☐ Other _____

Location: _____

People: _____

Objects and Things: _____

Colors: _____

Numbers: _____

Animals: _____

Actions: _____

Describe the Dream:

_____
_____
_____
_____
_____
_____
_____
_____
_____
_____
_____
_____

Dream Journal

Draw Your Dream:

Dream Meaning:

Notes:

Date: _____ Time: _____

Possible timeframe: ☐ Past ☐ Present ☐ Future ☐ Unknown

Feeling & Description: ☐ Happy ☐ Sad ☐ Anger

☐ Other _____

Location: _____

People: _____

Objects and Things: _____

Colors: _____

Numbers: _____

Animals: _____

Actions: _____

Describe the Dream:

_____
_____
_____
_____
_____
_____
_____
_____
_____
_____
_____
_____
_____

Dream Journal

Draw Your Dream:

Dream Meaning:

_____
_____
_____
_____
_____
_____
_____

Notes:

_____
_____
_____
_____
_____
_____
_____
_____

Notes

Notes

Notes

Notes

Notes

Notes

Notes

Notes

Notes

Notes

Notes

Notes

Notes

Notes

Notes

Notes

Notes

Notes

Notes

Notes

www.ingramcontent.com/pod-product-compliance
Lightning Source LLC
Chambersburg PA
CBHW071812080526
44589CB00012B/770